Special Olympics Georgia

Come be inspired...

Turner Publishing Company
Nashville, Tennessee • Paducah, Kentucky

Turner®
PUBLISHING COMPANY

412 Broadway • P.O. Box 3101
Paducah, Kentucky 42002-3101
(270) 443-0121

www.turnerpublishing.com

Turner Publishing Company Staff:
Darla Parrish, Editor
Shelley R. Davidson, Designer

Library of Congress Control No. 2004110597

ISBN: 1-59652-002-7

Printed in the United States of America

0 1 2 3 4 5 6 7 8 9

CONTENTS

"Let me win. But if I cannot win, let me be brave in the attempt." In keeping with the Special Olympics oath, every athlete receives a medal or a participant's ribbon for official competitions. Games are held in winter, spring, and summer on local, area, and state levels.

OUR MISSION STATEMENT

The mission of Special Olympics Georgia is to provide year-round sports training and athletic competition in a variety of Olympic-type sports for all children and adults with intellectual disabilities, giving them continuing opportunities to develop physical fitness, demonstrate courage, experience joy, and participate in the sharing of gifts, skills and friendship with their families, other Special Olympics athletes and the community.

In 1970, 500 athletes gathered at a suburban Atlanta college to participate in the first-ever track and field event held under the Special Olympics Georgia banner. During its first 35 years, the organization has grown exponentially and has helped thousands of children and adults in the process. The number of active athletes has grown to more than 22,000, participating in 23 sports.

Special Olympics is the first – and still the only – organization to offer training and competition for these athletes. The continuing success of the organization depends on your support and the ongoing support of the community.

We invite you to meet our athletes. Read their stories, see their courage and understand their extraordinary capabilities. These are the stories behind the Games of Special Olympics Georgia. Come be inspired by them.

Athlete's Oath:
"Let me win. But if I cannot win, let me be brave in the attempt."

1968 Special Olympics International begins in 1968 when Mrs. Eunice Kennedy Shriver organizes the First International Special Olympics Games at Soldier Field, Chicago, Illinois, USA.

1970 500 athletes gather at a suburban Atlanta college to participate in the first ever athletics event held under the Special Olympics Georgia banner.

1972 The Third International Special Olympics Summer Games take place at the University of California–Los Angeles with 2,500 participants.

1975 The Fourth International Special Olympics Summer Games take place at Central Michigan University in Mount. Pleasant, Michigan, with 3,200 athletes from 10 countries taking part. The Games are broadcast nationwide on CBS' "Sports Spectacular."

1977 The First International Special Olympics Winter Games are held in Steamboat Springs, Colorado, with more than 500 athletes competing in skiing and ice skating events. CBS, ABC, and NBC television networks cover the Games.

1979 The Fifth International Special Olympics Summer Games take place at the State University of New York at Brockport with more than 3,500 athletes from every state in the nation and more than 20 countries.

1983 The Sixth International Special Olympics Summer Games are held at Louisiana State University in Baton Rouge. A crowd of more than 60,000 attend the Opening Ceremony and approximately 4,000 athletes participate. Special Olympics Georgia sends a large delegation to the Games.

1985 Athletes from 14 countries are represented in skiing and skating events at the Third International Special Olympics Winter Games in Park City, Utah.

1987 More than 30,000 law enforcement officers from every state in the nation and seven countries run 26,000 miles in the Law Enforcement Torch Run® for Special Olympics. The 1987 Torch Run raises more than $2 million.

The University of Notre Dame and Saint Mary's College in South Bend, Indiana, host the Seventh International Special Olympics Summer Games. More than 4,700 athletes from more than 70 countries participate in 1987's largest amateur sports event. The Games. Special Olympics Georgia is part of the USA delegation.

Special Olympics Georgia introduces the Law Enforcement Torch Run (LETR) for the state of Georgia

1988 Special Olympics Unified Sports™ is launched at the annual Special Olympics Conference in Reno, Nevada.

1989 The Fourth International Special Olympics Winter Games are held in Reno, Nevada, and Lake Tahoe, California. More than 1,000 athletes from 18 countries participate. Special Olympics Georgia athletes and coaches are in attendance.

1991 The eighth Special Olympics World Summer Games are held in Minneapolis/St. Paul, Minnesota. Six thousand athletes from more than 100 countries make this the largest sporting event in the world in 1991. SOGA sent 105 athletes to contend in the summer games. Special Olympics Georgia has more than 16,000 athletes, 38,000 volunteers, and competes in 20 different Olympic-type sports.

1993 The fifth Special Olympics World Winter Games are held in Salzburg and Schladming, Austria, with 1,600 athletes from more than 50 countries participating in five winter sports. These are the first World Winter Games held outside North America. Special Olympics Georgia sends athletes in skating and alpine skiing.

1995 Special Olympics Georgia hosts the first annual Bob Busse Golf Tournament.

Over 7,000 athletes from 143 countries gather in New Haven, Connecticut, for competition in 21 sports at the ninth Special Olympics World Summer Games. 70 athletes representing Special Olympics Georgia participated in the World Games.

1996 UPS becomes a Special Olympics Georgia statewide partner after many years of support.

1997 Nearly 2,000 athletes from 73 countries compete in five Olympic-type winter sports in Toronto/Collingwood, Ontario, Canada for the sixth Special Olympics World Winter Games. This event is the world's largest winter multisport event in 1997. Special Olympics Georgia proudly sends three athletes and coaches.

1999 Special Olympics Georgia sends 116 athletes and coaches to the tenth Special Olympics World Summer Games held in the Raleigh, Durham and Chapel Hill area (Triangle) in North Carolina. Over 7,000 athletes representing 150 countries compete in 19 sports.

2001 Over 1,800 athletes representing approximately 70 countries compete in seven Olympic-type winter sports at the 2001 Special Olympics World Winter Games in Anchorage, Alaska. The 2001 Special Olympics World Winter Games are the largest sporting event ever

First-ever Global Youth Summit is held in conjunction with the 2001 Special Olympics World Winter Games. Thirty-four students with and without intellectual disabilities from around the world work in pairs to report on the World Games and discuss how to overcome obstacles and barriers to inclusion. A Special Olympics Georgia athlete attends the summit.

2003 Special Olympics continues to empower individuals with intellectual disabilities in over 150 countries worldwide.

The 2003 Special Olympics World Summer Games are held in Dublin, Ireland — the first Summer Games ever held outside the United States. The world's largest sporting event for 2003 featured 7,000 athletes from more than 50 countries participating in 21 sports.

2004 The number of athletes that participate in Special Olympics Georgia reaches 23,500, participating in 23 Olympic type events.

2005 Special Olympics Georgia is committed to growth of the organization, providing athletes with quality events, and generating widespread public awareness for the thousands who are involved, and those we invite to get involved.

Come Be Inspired...

action

Sometimes life's greatest challenges are life's greatest lessons.

SCOTT HEYMAN

Living with a sibling with special needs is one of God's greatest gifts and I am lucky to have Scott as my big brother. Scott has fragile X syndrome; the world's leading cause of mental impairment that is genetic. Without Scott, my family would not be nearly as interesting as we are today. The love and laughter that Scott brings to our family is immeasurable. He always has a smile on his face and is so excited to see you. His positive energy is contagious and rejuvenates everyone around him.

Yes, there are times when it is difficult living with a sibling with special needs, yet the bad times simply frame the good times. Scott has times when he gets so excited that he acts inappropriately in public; however, if you think about it, *everyone* has their moments. Also, there are times that our family may not be able to participate in certain activities because Scott does not want to, yet we still have fun hanging out together. Scott is more than a brother with special needs; Scott is the glue that brings my family closer in the most healthy and positive way.

Since the publication of my book, <u>My eXtra Special Brother: How to Love, Understand, and Celebrate your Sibling with Special Needs</u>, I have learned that not everyone sees children with special needs in the same way. Unfortunately, some people see their family members through the wrong set of lenses.

Imagine wearing glasses, "eXtra special glasses," that allow you to focus on the abilities of your loved ones, instead of their disability. These glasses are powerful; they enable you to see life in a more clear and brighter way. However, it is up to the eyes of the beholder to learn how to use these "eXtra special glasses" properly. Some people are born wearing these glasses, while others only find them later in life. These glasses come in all sizes and shapes, and they are effective if one is willing to give them a chance. And, the same colorful vision can be seen when living with a sibling with special needs.

One can view a brother or sister with special needs as an embarrassment or a shame to the family. They can choose to only focus on the negative and upsetting moments. However, if you put on your eXtra special corrective lenses, then you will see life differently. You can laugh at embarrassing moments and celebrate challenging experiences. Just because someone is different, does not mean they don't share in your same thoughts, feelings, and dreams. Sometimes life's greatest challenges are life's greatest lessons.

Life, as seen in the eyes of the beholder, can be quite special - so put on your "eXtra special glasses" and discover the joys of living with your sibling with special needs!

courage

Pat believes that Special Olympics played an important part in saving his life - and it has given him the opportunity to stay strong so that he could compete and win.

PATRICK MCDUFFIE

Patrick McDuffie is the kind of fellow that when he laughs you find you have no choice but to laugh with him. As a child he was diagnosed as autistic. However, Pat has never appreciated people who want to treat him differently from everyone else. He prefers to be given the opportunity to make his own way through life. If he fails, then he fails. Pat is the kind of person who gets back up and dusts himself off when he gets down and will then start over. This fighting spirit has served him well. In fact, this fighting spirit saved his life.

When Pat was a junior in high school, he was selected to become part of a horticultural program at the Fernbank Science Center in DeKalb County. In order to get to and from the program he had to ride the bus. Pat looked after some of the smaller kids that rode the bus with him. One day Pat was running late after class and the bus was early and he had to hurry so he could ride with the smaller kids that he helped. While he was crossing a busy street to catch the bus, all of his friends and fellow riders watched as Pat was hit by a truck.

He was transported to Dekalb General Hospital and seemed to be in good spirits but by the next morning he began to go into shock. The doctor making rounds that morning realized that Pat was developing fatty emboli. The fat from the bone marrow of his badly broken leg was getting into his blood stream and flowing to his lungs. Pat was put on pure oxygen and given packed cell blood. He was transferred to ICU but his heart rate soared to 160 and his temperature went over 100. They placed Pat on an ice mattress and he lapsed into semi-consciousness.

Then, things got worse – the medicine that Pat was given had to be discontinued because it was causing his lungs to bleed. Pat was on his own and was given little chance of survival. But, like I said before, Pat's fighting spirit served him well – it saved his life. Having his athletic background, he was in good shape and wouldn't give up. He fought for over two weeks and his doctors had even given up hope. Then, his heart rate and fever began to go down. At first, everyone thought that he was dying, but he began to talk. When he told the nurse that he was hungry, we knew

Pat was back. The doctors were amazed that Pat had survived and they called Pat, God's miracle.

Pat had a long way to go in order to recover. After a brief period of time for recuperation, Pat's badly broken leg had to be re-broken and holes had to be drilled into his leg so that six metal rods could be inserted. The doctors placed three rods above the break and three rods below the break so that a Hoffman device could be attached to the outside of his leg. Then there was therapy. But the injured leg would not respond because it had not been used for so long. Pat went through agony to try to get the leg to bend normally. A week later when the therapist had given up, Pat was sitting at the breakfast table with his knee fully bent - a second miracle.

When Pat walked across the stage at his high school graduation, the entire student body stood and cheered and gradually everyone else in the room did likewise. According to some of his classmates, Pat had become the most popular senior in his class because of his indomitable fighting spirit.

In February of 2001, Pat was the featured speaker during Developmental Disability Day at the Georgia State Capitol. He encouraged the Governor and members of the General Assembly to provide funding for Medicaid waivers. He told the Governor and the legislators that people with disabilities need the opportunity to be able to live and enjoy the same things as other Americans experience. The Governor, on several occasions, has spoken with Pat about supporting a bill approving a Special Olympics Georgia automobile tag.

Pat is now 41 years old. He works at the Emory University Conference Center where he is not only an important team member of the staff but is considered a special ambassador. Pat still competes in Special Olympics as a swimmer. He speaks to groups as a Global Messenger for Special Olympics. He enjoys speaking to different groups on behalf of Special Olympics, telling his story and encouraging others to support Special Olympics Georgia. Pat believes that Special Olympics Georgia played an important part in saving his life and has given him the opportunity to stay strong so he could compete and win on and off the playing field of life.

Stephanie has seen and done things we would never have dreamed she was capable of, all because of Special Olympics Georgia.

STEPHANIE CONNELLY

Stephanie had her first seizure when she was two-months-old. She was flown by Life Flight from what was then Walton County Hospital to Children's Healthcare of Atlanta. Seeing the helicopter lift off with our precious little girl was the loneliest, most helpless feeling I had ever experienced. It was only the beginning of several unanswered questions and endless searching for help and fervent prayers. Six years later, an answer came, when Stephanie's special education teacher signed Stephanie up for the Special Olympics local games.

The first real turning point came in middle school when the local coordinator for Walton County Special Olympics became Stephanie's special education teacher. She tutored Stephanie after school in reading, but also she challenged her to compete against other runners in Special Olympics competition. She ran the four hundred and eight hundred-meter races.

While running at the high school track one evening, the high school cross-country coach invited Stephanie to join his team. She out ran everyone at the State Fall Games in the one-mile race. Coach signed her up for the track and cross country teams the following year. Stephanie's junior year, she placed second in the region in both cross country and long distance running. She went from just another special education student to a member of a regional championship team and it all started with Special Olympics…but the story doesn't end here.

Because she became such a strong runner, in 1999 Stephanie was invited to the Special Olympics World Summer Games in Raleigh, North Carolina. With seven thousand athletes from one hundred and fifty countries around the world, she was asked to run a half-marathon. I thought it was too much to ask her to do, but her coaches thought otherwise. We began Stephanie's training and on June 25, 1999, she flew on a leer jet with Team USA to Raleigh. In the ninety degree heat on July 4th, forty plus friends and family, including the local Special Olympics coordinator, her high school track coach, and members of Harmony Baptist Church cheered as she crossed the finish line. She won a silver medal in the thirteen mile race. For a child that could not walk alone until she was seventeen-months-old…this was quite an accomplishment!

That year, with training from Special Olympics, Stephanie learned self-confidence and independence. We learned to never doubt her abilities and we realized that God had used Special Olympics to show us her hidden talents.

Stephanie thrived with her renewed self-esteem and it showed in her school work. Instead of sitting at home with nothing to do, watching while her sister was going out with friends and chatting on the phone; Special Olympics gave Stephanie her own claim to fame. She became a Global Messenger for Special Olympics Georgia, which got her involved with the Law Enforcement Torch Run. She fell in love with all of the officers, and they invited her to run in a relay marathon at Myrtle Beach, South Carolina. While training she ran a road race in Plains, Georgia, and was presented her second place trophy by former President Jimmy Carter.

Stephanie has seen and done things we would have never dreamed she was capable of, all because of Special Olympics. Special Olympics Georgia has inspired greatness in Stephanie and she has inspired others. Now, at age 22, Stephanie helps train new runners, holds a job in a day care at the Walton Medical Fitness Center, attends Athens Technical School, volunteers at Walton Regional Medical Center, and helps teach pre-schoolers at Harmony Baptist Church.

All of this began with the feelings of pride, accomplishment and self-esteem gained through Special Olympics. Special Olympics changed the way others…teachers, friends, employers and her own parents saw Stephanie. Special Olympics has been an answer to our prayers.

inspire

She delights in demonstrating
that "Down" can be "Up"!
It all depends on your
perspective!

CYNTHIA OUTMAN

Cynthia Outman is a very determined young lady. She began her education at the young age of three months in DeKalb County's Parent-Infant Program. Cynthia completed Parent-Infant and Early Childhood Special Education classes at Coralwood Special Education Center.

At age six, Cynthia was mainstreamed for Kindergarten. For grades one through seven, she was in special education classes for academics and inclusive classes for physical education, music, and art. She was also mainstreamed for extracurricular activities so that she might benefit from modeling "normal" peers: piano, tap, ballet, jazz dance, and Brownies. She was a Metropolitan Atlanta "Poster Child" and national "Special Ambassador" for the March of Dimes.

Cynthia attended both inclusive and special needs summer camps. She took part in activities for special athletes: karate, tennis, soccer, basketball, softball, and bowling. She competed in Special Olympics in aquatics, alpine skiing, ice skating, roller skating, and equestrian events, winning 8 bronze medals, 18 silver medals, and 51 gold medals.

During most of her years in high school, Cynthia's schedule included two special education self-contained classes, two resource classes, and two inclusive classes. When she was interested in taking Child Care her senior year, one of the program heads was skeptical and said, "No one with Down Syndrome has ever done it." When I told Cynthia his comment, she responded "Well, I guess I'll just have to show him, Mom!" Cynthia passed the entrance test. In fact, the department head admitted later that she scored the highest anyone had ever scored on the fine motor dexterity portion. Cynthia completed the course with a "B" average. Her inner drive and ambition contributed much toward her success.

In order to get a "regular" diploma, it was necessary for Cynthia to pass the Georgia High School Graduation test. It took her four times, but she passed it just in time to graduate with her class in June of 1996, with honors. Cynthia was awarded the HOPE Scholarship and received an Award for Educational Excellence from President Clinton.

Cynthia was determined to go to college and become a teacher's aide. DeKalb Technical Institute offered a course in early childhood paraprofessional training. When it came time to begin paraprofessional courses, she was met with resistance. The Program Head and associate teacher tried to dissuade her. Cynthia and I discussed the program and how difficult it was going to be if she pursued it. I told her it was her decision. Cynthia said, "Mom, remember how the program head didn't think I could do Child Care? Well, I showed him, and I will show these teachers, too. I want to take this course!" True to her word, Cynthia "made believers" of the teachers by the end of the first year.

She did her student teaching in the spring of 1999. She completed the program after twelve quarters of study with more elective hours than she needed to graduate. Cynthia graduated from DeKalb Technical Institute with a diploma in the Education Paraprofessional Training Course on September 23, 1999. Her final GPA was 3.28. In January of 2000, she began her paraprofessional career at Coralwood School.

Her career is very important to her, but Cynthia still loves her free time. She has an active social life with her friends and her boyfriend. She loves to travel and especially likes cruises. She continues to work in her church and community. She served on the Board of the Georgia Advocacy Office and as a "Global Messenger" for Special Olympics. She has a special love for speaking to groups about the positive aspects of Down Syndrome. She delights in demonstrating that "Down can be Up! It all depends on your perspective!"

Cynthia enjoys going to concerts and plays. For the past two years, she herself has been performing in Habima Theater plays, most recently as the leading lady in "Music Man, Junior." Her next goal is "to live independently in an apartment with a roommate or maybe even a husband." I am sure it will happen . . . there's no reason to believe otherwise.

Special Olympics Georgia is adding a dimension to life that only one generation ago was completely out of reach for special populations.

RAY BRENNAN

Ray is a very pleasant and personable young man. One of his greatest accomplishments is his continuous employment since high school. Currently, he is a grounds keeper at Emory University in Atlanta. This is quite an achievement as Ray has always been reluctant to try anything new. Once he is shown that he can do something, he is confident and works independently.

Ray's ability to do this is a direct result of his involvement in Special Olympics. He has learned that one must work to accomplish a complicated task. He has learned from his softball pitching that it takes practice, practice and more practice to "get it right." These skills have been instrumental in helping him to succeed in work-related tasks.

Ray has always been afraid of horses, but you would never know it watching him ride in Atlanta's Peach Bowl Parade. Even though he is still afraid of his horse, Chip, it doesn't stop him from getting up on Chip and leading him through a program. He would never have had that feeling of achievement without someone helping him to overcome his fears. This translates directly to Ray's work. One of Ray's major tasks is to control a very large industrial lawnmower with his 5 foot 2 inch body. Who better to teach this than a 500 pound horse?

Ray enjoys his work immensely and feels great pride in what he does. He has a very strong feeling of commitment and takes pride in keeping Emory University beautiful. Without Special Olympics, he would not have developed skills that allowed him to contribute to mainstream society.

Thanks to his participation in swimming, ice skating, tennis, horseback riding, track, volleyball, softball and bowling, Ray enjoys a large circle of friends. He is quite a busy guy, and always has a smile.

That smile comes from doing something you love with friends. This does not end on the courts, lanes or fields. It continues with the phone conversations about how the team is doing. Here again, Special Olympics is adding a dimension to life that only one generation ago was completely out of reach for special populations.

Ray epitomizes the expression "be all that you can be" and Special Olympics Georgia has played a major part in his success.

courage

She has learned that whether she wins the gold, or comes in last – giving it her all is what matters the most.

BETH BRIDGERS

Beth Bridgers is a thirty-year-old young lady that lives in Smyrna, Georgia, with her parents, Joe and Betsy Bridgers. Beth works as a courtesy clerk at Publix Supermarkets. She graduated from Osborne High School in 1993.

The summer after graduation, Beth learned about Special Olympics from two friends. She joined the softball team, and until then, had never played ball or been part of a team. But she soon found out that she could do it.

Her first trip to the State Tournament had to be played inside with plastic bats and wiffle balls because it rained the whole weekend. Despite bad weather, Beth made the best of it and met lots of new friends. She also won her first silver medal!

When softball ended, she became a cheerleader for the Special Olympics basketball team in Cobb County. She had always wanted to be a cheerleader – and at last she was a cheerleader! Not only was her team the only cheerleading squad at the State Winter Games but they even got their picture in the newspaper!

Next, Beth joined the Cobb County swim team. Her coach was always telling her, "Kick your feet, kick your feet." The advice helped, and that's where she won her first GOLD medal!

In 1995, she started participating in equestrian events. She really loves horses and understands that taking care of a horse is hard work, but so is riding! Beth even got her very own horse in 1998, Miss Sandy Gin! In 1999, she was selected to be a member of Team Georgia's equestrian team and compete in the Special Olympics World Summer Games in Raleigh, North Carolina.

Special Olympics has added to her life in so many ways. Through all of her practices, Beth gets plenty of exercise, travels extensively and meets many new friends at each event. She has learned that winning gold or coming in last, what matters most is giving it her all. At the end of the day, nothing that she truly wants to achieve is out of her reach.

Beth was asked to be a Global Messenger for Special Olympics Georgia. She really enjoys getting to talk to people and share her stories of what Special Olympics has given her.

joy

**Special Olympics
Georgia gave him the
gift of opportunity.**

ALFRED COLE

Alfred grew up in Dallas, Georgia, where he attended Paulding County High School. After high school, Alfred got a job at the Bartow County workshop. At the workshop, Alfred worked on a cement contract job. He lived with his mother until he turned 21. Alfred then moved to the Brookrun Campus, where he lived for eight years. At Brookrun, Alfred made many friends, worked in a sheltered workshop and participated in Special Olympics softball, bowling and athletics.

At age 29, Alfred moved into an even more independent living situation with Resources and Residential Alternatives, Incorporated. There, he shared an apartment with one other roommate and his House Manager. When Alfred had been living at the apartment for a few years, the complex caught fire. He and his roommates lost almost all their belongings. Since then, he has moved into a group home, which is also managed by Resources and Residential Alternatives, but he now has a big backyard that he loves!

Alfred has had several jobs out in the community since he's been with Resources and Residential Alternatives. He is very proud of the fact that he obtained his current job with no assistance from the staff! His current job is at the Brunswick Bowling Center in Roswell, Georgia, where he works as a customer service representative. Alfred says that he really likes living where everyone treats him well and he has a lot of freedom to do the things he enjoys.

Some of the things Alfred enjoys most are tennis, golf and going on vacation. Having won hundreds of medals, ribbons and trophies, Alfred is a very gifted athlete and is often asked to travel for competitions. In 2003, he went to the Special Olympics World Summer Games in Dublin, Ireland, to represent the state of Georgia in both the singles and doubles tennis competition. Alfred came home with the Gold Medal! He has also participated in the Regional Special Olympics Golf Tournament in Port Saint Lucie, Florida. He feels fortunate to have been able to go on so many fun trips. Some of the places he has gone are Las Vegas, New Orleans and Panama City.

Another favorite pastime of Alfred's is being able to spend time with his friend, Tom. Alfred refers to Tom as his father figure. Alfred had a very difficult time after his mother died. Although he has four brothers and three sisters, he says it is difficult to keep in touch with all his family members because they all are busy working just like he is. He and Tom share a love of golf, which they play often! Tom also makes sure Alfred is included in all of his family's holiday gatherings.

Special Olympics has been honored in the past to have Alfred serve as a Global Messenger. In that position, he gave several speeches, but his first speech was about opportunity – because that's what Special Olympics gave him.

Alfred's future goal is to work toward earning his GED. When Alfred accomplishes that goal, he would love to go to college! His dream is to become a doctor, a lawyer or a plumber… he is just not sure which!

inspire

She has a smile that will warm your heart and the courage of a lion.

ALICIA BRAY

Alicia Bray is a remarkable twenty-six-year-old young lady from Douglasville, Georgia. She has a smile that will warm your heart and the courage of a lion.

When you first meet Alicia you would never realize how amazing it is that she is even alive. Alicia's mother, Carmen, was in a nearly fatal car accident when she was six months pregnant with Alicia. The accident happened on April 22, 1978, when Carmen was twenty-years-old and was coming back from a wedding. Alicia was born the next day.

The accident left Carmen physically disabled and Alicia was born profoundly deaf and later needed eyeglasses. Alicia's grandmother, Florence, a remarkable woman, raised her.

I first met Alicia in the fall of 1996 at Deer Lick Park in Douglasville. Florence brought her to a special needs basketball program in hopes Alicia would be interested. I didn't know sign language, but Alicia taught me the basic signs.

We immediately bonded and she faithfully showed up for basketball practice every week. She was a blessing to have on the team. Alicia was always eager to learn and always happy to play. I could be having the worst day, but when I worked with her and the other athletes they had a way of making me feel better.

Alicia always competed in the local track and field competition in Douglasville, Georgia. But she never attended State Games until the fall of 2001. She started to play for the Douglas County Blue Dragons Softball team. In the fall of 2002, Alicia started competing in Bocce on a State level, and she is still involved in bocce, as well as bowling.

Alicia has reached so many goals and has such an active life. She works two hours a day at Babies R Us. In her spare time, Alicia loves to swim and take care of her animals. Her pets include one dog, three cats and two beta fish. Florence will tell you that those animals are Alicia's responsibility as well as her pride and joy—just as Alicia and Carmen are Florence's pride and joy. They all live together to this day- one happy family sharing each other's triumphs, victories and challenges. That's what life is all about.

Special Olympics Georgia has truly opened the world to Dennis.

DENNIS DAVIS

Less than five years ago a social worker asked me to join a meeting with Dennis and his older brother, Ron. Ron was gathering information to let Dennis continue to live in his childhood home. Ron also wanted to find out how Dennis could meet others and have something valuable outside the home—that's where I came in.

I stood in the room and listened to Ron describe how much he wanted "Denny" to live as normally as possible. He wanted Denny to remain in the house his parents had owned and he wanted him to become a part of his community. As I listened to Ron speak, I watched as Dennis sat quietly, occasionally looking at his brother and when prompted replied with a very quiet, "Yeah." Ron suggested Dennis could volunteer with Special Olympics Georgia. I then caught Ron by surprise when I said he could compete as an athlete. Ron was puzzled and replied, "In what?"

None of us could have ever predicted the influence that one simple suggestion would have. Dennis is an adult who is intellectually disabled and has hemiparesis that affects his left arm and leg. With his quiet demeanor, it is sometimes easy to forget he is there. I admit it has happened to me. The first sport he tried was bocce. He attended weekly practices with the team and slowly got to know everyone. As we drove to the State Fall Games competition, he sat directly behind the driver's seat; my seat. I stopped to drop the bocce athletes off at their venue for divisioning, and quickly left to get the softball team to their venue. As we got to the other side of town I suddenly realized Dennis was still in the van with me! Although we were unable to return to bocce I was able to take care of the situation, but I told Dennis next time he needed to speak up if he knew there was a problem. As it turned out, I would often encourage Dennis to speak up.

Since then, Dennis has competed in bowling, basketball and badminton. Bocce has become his best sport. His highest honor came when he was selected to represent the United States at the 2003 Special Olympics World Summer Games in Dublin, Ireland. Dennis not only improved his game, but more importantly he proved to everyone, and himself, he could be a vital member of a team. During the course of the competitions, Dennis improved to the point he was able to hit where he aimed. Many people feel that winning the gold medal with his unified partner was his biggest accomplishment, and I would have to agree, it was amazing to watch. It was also amazing to see him win bronze in the Unified Team competition and silver in the Individual competition. But the greatest moment to me, was when this soft-spoken person, who shows little facial emotions, broke out into a <u>huge</u> smile when he made a great shot. At that point, I believe, Dennis realized his importance.

Recently, I spoke with Ron about Dennis' accomplishments. Ron recalled the time we were introduced, "I will never forget that day, you looked at Dennis and immediately wanted him on your team. I couldn't imagine him participating in any sport." Ron's views about his brother have changed significantly. His advice to Dennis now is, "You can do what ever you want. You're a champion. You have a gold medal to prove it!"

Dennis continues to be an important member of our team. After returning from the World Games he became somewhat of a celebrity as he was featured on the local television news and in the newspaper. Although still soft spoken, he will call me to ask about practices and the State Games. Special Olympics Georgia has truly opened the world to Dennis!

courage

It would be hard to imagine Clay Doub's life without Special Olympics Georgia.

CLAY DOUB

When Clay Doub first started participating in Special Olympics, he was a very shy first grader who would not look anyone in the eye. Now, Clay is a 25-year-old young adult who never meets a stranger. He is still very much involved in Special Olympics Georgia.

Currently, Clay works for the City of Valdosta Parks and Recreation Department. He also attends adult literacy classes two nights a week and speech therapy at Valdosta State University.

Special Olympics has been a major reason Clay has developed into an outgoing adult athlete. Clay has received numerous medals in floor hockey, bowling, swimming, softball, equestrian, athletics and volleyball. In 1995, Clay received the prestigious Naismith Award for Special Olympics Basketball Athlete of the Year for the state of Georgia. The Atlanta Tip-off Club presented this award to him at the World Congress Center in Atlanta. He then received the 1998 Achievement Award from the Mayor's Council for Person's with Disabilities.

Not only has Special Olympics helped Clay develop physically, but mentally as well. Through all of these activities and sports, Clay has learned people skills and has been able to experience things most people experience in everyday life. This has helped him become comfortable going on trips away from home with a group. His incredible experiences are endless. Without Special Olympics, his involvement in organized sports would have been little, if any. It would be hard to imagine Clay Doub's life without Special Olympics Georgia.

joy

That's *my son* they are cheering for!

JUDSON ENRIGHT

"That's my son. That's *my son* they are cheering for," recalled Judson's mother, as she recounted the first time Judson competed at the Special Olympics Georgia State Games. Judson was competing in the fifteen meter walk for Level A Aquatics. "I will never forget that moment," she continued. In fact, it was a special day for Judson and both his parents. Coaching Judson is only part of the reason I was there that day; I am also his father.

Judson has not always had the opportunity to be included, for most of his life he had been separated from others. From age four to eighteen, he lived in a residential facility where he existed in his "own little world." Judson has many factors against him; he is autistic and profoundly mentally challenged with mild cerebral palsy. He is non-verbal and suffers seizures daily. Judson has also had a curvature of his spine surgically repaired. He had always been the person who was never picked for the team.

Now, 17 years later, he may still live in his own world, but he is able to rent his own home and he is part of a team. One of Judson's favorite activities is playing in the water. Although he cannot swim, the pool has been very beneficial for him, I taught him how to walk by using the pool.

The pool, along with Special Olympics Georgia, made him part of a team. The year was 2001; he went to the Special Olympics Georgia Summer Games at Emory University. At age 23, Judson was attending his first state competition. He traveled with the team from Augusta to Atlanta on a Thursday. It would be a long time until his competition on Sunday.

As a member of the team, he was expected to go with the others wherever they went. As the head coach, I had double duty at the Games. I was in charge of the team, but also had to take care of Judson when his mom was unavailable. Although it meant getting up earlier, feeding Judson at the meals, and always having him near me, I would not have missed it. This was his moment to shine! Judson did great during the games. He kept up better than many of the other athletes. The days were long, and he went to sleep with little difficulty.

Sunday finally arrived and our two months of practices were about to pay off. Judson and I slipped into the water. The starter began the race and Judson stood in place taking in the whole situation. It took what felt like an eternity for him to start walking across the pool. Once he got started, he kept going until the end where he and I gave each other a big hug. As I lifted him onto the deck of the pool I spotted his mom who was very proud and emotional. I, too, was feeling the emotions. One of the coolest days of my life was to see Judson presented with a silver medal. At that moment, I realized everyone was cheering for Judson. Our son had become a champion!

His stature is mountainous, but he has a gentle, giving spirit just as immense.

Arnold "P.G." Griffin

At first glance, he would intimidate most, a giant of a man with a deep resonant voice that echoes his own strength. Standing 6 feet 3 inches tall and weighing 275 pounds, his stature is mountainous, but he has a gentle, giving spirit just as immense. In a phrase, P.G. Griffin is simply larger than life.

The first time I met Arnold Griffin, ("P.G." as he is affectionately known) he reminded me of the legendary figure John Henry, a heroic man who was said to have died with his steel hammer in his hand proving a human being is better than a machine. Like John Henry, P.G.'s character is equally as noble. He has many dimensions of who he is; athlete, minister and mentor among others. He's an accomplished athlete and has won more than 600 medals.

In 1999, P.G. was chosen to go to the Special Olympics World Summer Games in Raleigh, North Carolina. It was there that he set two new world records in powerlifting. One was a dead lift of 650.75 pounds.

Equally as compelling is P.G.'s spiritual commitment and doing good works. Chatting with him last May at the State Summer Games, he paused to answer his cell phone to offer some encouraging words to the young lady on the other end of the line. "I have a lot of friends I have to pray for and a lot of churches that I deal with and volunteer my time. And that's the greatest feeling," he said. "As a minister, every day, I'm going to carry God with me wherever I go." In fact, I recently found out why he goes by the initials "P.G."—P.G. means "Praise God."

I've also been able to observe P.G. as an incredible mentor. The other Special Olympics athletes idolize him, he really is a celebrity to them. He comes to many Special Olympics Georgia events, visiting each venue, just talking with people, shaking hands, and signing autographs. "It's all about Special Olympics, bringing people to Special Olympics. And when I go train, help train some of the kids… I just try to have a good attitude…And you just got to be for real. You know, what comes in your heart, what goes out of your heart. And any little kids that I see, I try to be there for them," he said in a 2002 interview for CNN's "Sunday Morning."

When I meet remarkable people like P.G., and I think of John Henry, I think of how the railroad workers said John Henry couldn't outpace that steam-powered rock drill, and how he courageously proved his detractors wrong. P.G. proved his doubters wrong, too. Today he is a champion. The thought buoys my spirit, and I know that the work we do at Special Olympics Georgia is not in vain.

action

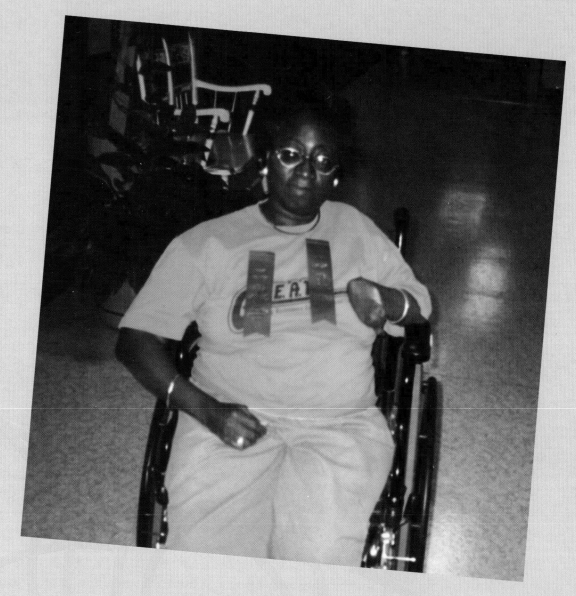

She has a contagious personality and an unforgettable laugh.

BOBBIE JEAN HALL

Bobbie Jean Hall, also known as B.J., was born on May 5, 1959, in Baxley, Georgia. She was involved in an automobile accident with her mother when she was only 6-months-old. She was hospitalized in Augusta, Georgia, for some time after the accident. She has since experienced delays in meeting her developmental milestones. From the accident, Bobbie Jean has paralysis of the left side, severe contracture of the legs, seizure disorder, scoliosis, and an intellectual disability. She is also legally blind, but she wears glasses.

Bobbie Jean lived with her aunt until her aunt was placed into a nursing home. She currently lives alone in a housing authority in Glenville, Georgia. Even though she is wheelchair bound, she can get out and crawl around while at home. Bobbie Jean is very independent and can take care of most of her daily living skills.

Bobbie Jean began at the Tattnall-Evans Service Center on June 28, 1973. Today, she attends the center five days a week, six hours a day. Bobbie Jean works very hard in the workshop completing contracts that help to assemble lawn mowers. She has a contagious personality and an unforgettable laugh.

Bobbie Jean has always been interested in participating in Special Olympics. When she hears someone say "Special Olympics," she wheels down the hall with fist balled up yelling, "Yeah, Yeah, Yeah!" For the remainder of the day, she has a grin on her face.

From participating in Special Olympics, Bobbie Jean has gained the self confidence to practice as hard as she can in order to compete against other athletes. From her weekly practices, she has made friends with others at the center as well as meeting athletes at area games. Bobbie Jean is also a leader at practices. Since she has experience in Special Olympics, she helps out other athletes and coaches with preparing for practices and cheers on the other participants. Bobbie Jean not only motivates herself, but she motivates others around her.

Bobbie Jean competed in the International Special Olympics Summer Games that were held in Baton Rouge at Louisiana State University in July of 1983. She won a gold medal during the 30-meter Wheelchair Slalom and also competed and won a silver medal in the 25 meter Wheelchair Dash. She competed with 4,200 other athletes from 52 countries.

When Bobbie Jean was asked to talk about her Special Olympics memories, she paused and then began. "I just love it," she said. She added that winning a medal made her feel good. She said she has competed in the Special Olympics since she began at the center.

I asked Bobbie Jean to tell me about her experience when she went to Baton Rouge. Bobbie Jean said, "I was scared to fly because it was my first time ever. I got to Louisiana and after my competition, I toured the city," she said. A ladies' auxiliary group from Baton Rouge learned that one thing Bobbie Jean wanted was a camera - and they bought her one while she was there.

Bobbie Jean was able to meet a variety of celebrities while in Louisiana. She met some of the cast from 'Little House on the Prairie' and 'Dukes of Hazard'. She was also able to see Artie Johnson and Susan St. James while competing in the Special Olympics State Summer Games in Warner Robbins, Georgia in 1982. There, she won blue ribbons for both the 25 meter and 30 meter Wheelchair Slaloms. She still has her ribbons, medals, and autographs in a memory album.

Once Bobbie Jean returned, a reception was held for her in her hometown of Glennville. The public was invited to attend the reception and show their excitement for Bobbie Jean's accomplishments. The mayor of Glennville announced that Wednesday, October 5th, 1983, would become Bobbie Jean Hall Day.

Bobbie Jean, in her spare time, likes to go bowling and go to church. She also loves to help others and attends exercise classes twice a week. She is a very loving person who has benefited from her participation in Special Olympics. She has met her goal of winning medals and made friendships that will last a lifetime. Bobbie Jean is a motivator and has inspired a lot of competitors with her bright outlook on life.

courage

We don't all have to be the world's greatest at what we do...we try our absolute hardest and celebrate life's everyday happiness.

JASON HARE

Several times throughout the weekend of my first Special Olympics Georgia State Summer Games, I saw one particular athlete, Jason Hare. I can still bring the picture of him to mind, he had on a blue t-shirt and a red bandana around his neck. He is an athlete with cerebral palsy. His motions were awkward and seemed to require great effort. He was always with a coach who helped him. The coach would drive the wheelchair using the joystick on the arm and would make sure the athlete had all that he needed. I remember wondering just what Jason did during the Special Olympics. What did he 'take away' from his time with Special Olympics Georgia? He was obviously severely disabled and could not do much on his own. I wondered about how he practiced his sport and what life must be like for him.

As I walked down to the track to take in some of the races, I saw several athletes in electric wheelchairs heading to the staging area. Jason was among them. I remember thinking how odd that was – surely those athletes weren't going to race in their wheelchairs. I assumed all of the events would be on foot or with a manual wheelchair – what would a race be when all of the participants were moved by the battery in their electric chairs. The people who were lining up would be classified as severely disabled. My curiosity was peaked so I headed to the stands to watch.

The athletes lined up on the track. Lanes had been marked off with cones and were wider than they were for foot races. The athletes were brought up to the starting line; most were helped by their coach or assistant coach. The athletes weren't even guiding themselves at that point. I remember thinking that everyone would cross the finish line at the same time. After all, they were all in electric wheelchairs. This would be a very quick race and I didn't quite see where the competition would come in during this event, but I continued to watch with curiosity.

The gun went off and with jerking motions, starts and stops, the athletes headed down the track. After just a moment it became clear - this was not going to be a quick, easy race. It took every ounce of effort those athletes had to keep their hands on the sticks that drove their chairs. They had to work very hard to go forward – not even straight forward, just in the general direction of the finish line. The athletes had to stay in their lanes. Even with the additional space several had a hard time keeping within their boundaries.

My eyes were on Jason the whole time. I watched as he concentrated, putting so much effort into making his hands and arms do what his mind was telling them to do. He could see the finish line, but often headed more to the side than straight. The race went on and on. Athletes had to stop often to re-group, gaining control and then continuing.

I don't remember how long the race took – I know it was a long time. I don't even remember who won the gold. I do remember that each and every athlete crossed the finish line among cheers and shouts of encouragement. I remember seeing the faces of the coaches and the parents as they went from biting their nails with anticipation to jumping for joy with excitement that their athlete had completed the race, crossing the finish line all on their own.

Most of all, I remember Jason. He raised his arms above his head with the biggest smile I have ever seen. He laughed and laughed. It wasn't that he was first or that he had a perfect race or any of the things you might think sports is about. He crossed the finish line. He achieved his goal. He was given an opportunity to be something all on his own in a setting that was challenging but not impossible for him to be successful. Special Olympics is a place where he's accepted but moreover where he's EXPECTED to do his personal best – whatever that is - to succeed. There was no 'gimme' in this race. Everyone's achievements were significant that day.

I stood motionless for quite a while, taking it all in. I learned more from those athletes and especially from Jason than I have learned in a long time. It stays with me, reminding me that we don't all have to be the world's greatest at what we do. We have to set goals, try our absolute hardest and celebrate life's everyday happiness. It wasn't the battery on the wheelchair that got Jason across that line; it was his determination and skill that took him to the finish. I had missed so much with my first glance at those athletes. I made an assumption like a lot of people do, because he is disabled, "What can he do?" Now, I know I should have asked, "What can't he do?"

joy

Becca can certainly move emotions and influence opinions.

Rebecca "Becca" Ayers

Becca is a beautiful 17-year-old young lady with Spina Bifida. She is very close to my heart and a true inspiration to every one that knows her.

I was Becca's teacher for 5 1/2 years, and in that time, I learned the true meaning of inspiration. Webster defines inspiration as "the action or power of moving the intellect or emotions." Webster also states that inspiration is "the act of influencing or suggesting opinions." Becca's "abilities" can certainly move emotions and influence opinions.

Becca has a very supportive family–2 brothers, Josh and Stephen, mom and dad. They have always taken care of Becca without feeling sorry for her. When you feel sorry for someone with a disability, you aren't able to give him or her what they need. You aren't able to help them by feeling sorry for them. Becca's family has been very supportive, while teaching and allowing her to become the independent person that she is.

Becca has had multiple surgeries throughout her life and is at risk daily for infections in her body. However, nothing seems to deter her from living life to its fullest. Her favorite song is "I Believe I Can Fly" from the movie Space Jam. One day in class we asked the students to share, and sing if they would like, their favorite song. Becca did sing, "I believe I can fly. I believe I can touch the sky. I think about it every night and day, spread my wings and fly away. I believe I can soar. I see me running through that open door. I believe I can fly." That day, she moved my intellect. Right then and there I understood that Becca knows that there is a "light at the end of the tunnel" and she will not give up until she reaches it.

In middle school, Becca participated in Special Olympics events such as bowling and athletics. It was so great to see the smile on her face as she rolled the bowling ball off the ramp and knocked down the pins. Even to see her give all she had to get to that finish line in the wheelchair race. It was as if those imaginary wings carried her right across that finish line as she pushed those wheels. Becca also participated on a wheelchair basketball team and in swimming at the local YMCA.

Becca continues to compete in Special Olympics events. She has attended several State Games, competing in bowling and aquatics. She competes in bowling and athletics on the local and area levels. She is a truly remarkable young lady. She turns her disabilities into challenges and competes daily to defeat them. If you ever meet her, you will never be the same or view life in the same way.

The power to move the intellect or emotions? Yes, Becca has that power. The act of influencing opinions? Yes, Becca has that too. She is inspiration. She is Becca Ayers.

inspire

**Special Olympics
Georgia has taught me
that no matter what
anyone says, I am
somebody and I can
make a difference.**

TODD HOWARD

Todd K. Howard is a Special Olympics athlete in the state of Georgia. He began participating in Special Olympics in 1981 at Hahira Middle School in Hahira, Georgia. As a young athlete, there were many things that Todd had yet to learn.

In the beginning, some of the most valuable things he learned were skills in sports such as volleyball, basketball and floor hockey. As Todd moved on through school, he also moved on participating in Special Olympics. He began to learn the importance of teamwork and a good attitude. When Todd arrived at Lowndes High School, he continued with the same sports. By this time, he was practically a pro! But the fun didn't stop there. Todd graduated high school in 1987 and went to Warm Springs, Georgia to the Franklin D Roosevelt Institute.

While there, he was in horticulture training for the future work force. Todd was a little nervous but after his experience traveling with Special Olympics, he was somewhat prepared. When his training finished, they offered him a job at Callaway Gardens. There, he helped plant flowers and shrubs and maintain the grounds. When he finished training at Warm Springs, he went back home. Once he returned home, he got a job at Valdosta State University. (VSU)

On July 5, 1988, Todd became a member of the VSU grounds crew, and he is very proud to say that he is still there today—15 years later. When Todd rides his bicycle to work in the morning, he enjoys the time to think and get some fresh air. From planting in the flowerbeds to edging the sidewalks, it all means everything to him. After finishing his day's work, he can stand back and see the results. Todd truly loves his job!

In the 15 years that he's been employed at VSU, Todd has won two awards. In 1989, he won 'Best Handicapped Employee' in the state of Georgia. Then in 1998, he won 'Employee of the Year' for the Mayor's Council for Persons with Disabilities. Todd is especially proud of these two accomplishments.

Although he works a full time job, he still finds the time to participate in Special Olympics. After all, he says, "I would not be where I am today if it were not for the lessons learned with Special Olympics Georgia."

Through the years after high school Todd has added a few more sports like softball, bowling and badminton. He also became a Global Messenger for Special Olympics Georgia. As a Global Messenger, Todd went to Lowndes High School to speak with Special Education classes and encourage them to participate in Special Olympics. Todd says, "I explain to them that they can do anything they want to do if they put their mind to it. I also tell them that just because they're different, that doesn't mean they can't do anything."

"Also as a Global Messenger, I have spoken to various radio stations about not using the word "retarded", I explain to them that as a person with a disability I much prefer the words "intellectually disabled." I enjoy doing this because not everyone has the ability to voice their concerns or opinions and I love to help those that can't speak for themselves."

"In the past two years, I have also served as the athlete spokesperson on the Management Team for Valdosta. That puts me in the position to also voice the concerns of the athletes. It allows me to make any suggestions that athletes may have."

Todd says, "After 23 years, numerous State Games, 7 gold medals, 4 silver medal, 6 bronze medals and indescribable fun, I can honestly say that Special Olympics has been a major part of my life. Sure the dances are fun, the girls are pretty, it's fun to meet new friends, and it's always great to win, but it's so much more than that. Special Olympics has taught me to believe in myself and in what I can be. Special Olympics Georgia has taught me that no matter what anyone says, I am somebody and I can make a difference."

action

This is a family that brings attention to the needs of people with intellectual disabilities and helps to improve their lives – one step at a time.

NANDI ISAAC

Nandi Isaac totally embodies the athlete oath: *Let me win. But if I cannot win, let me be brave in the attempt.* Nandi is legally blind. Her family moved to Macon to be near the Georgia Academy for the Blind, where Nandi is a student. She also attends Central High School.

Nandi displays great courage when it comes to sports. In Special Olympics, Nandi participates in many sports including: equestrian, basketball team skills, tennis, softball, ice-skating and bocce. Ice-skating is one of Nandi's most recent interests and would seem to be most frightening with the prospect of falling for someone who doesn't see well. Nandi has never been afraid and seems to succeed in whatever she sets her mind to.

She recently traveled to Huntsville, Alabama, to compete in the Southeast Regional Ice-Skating Competition against athletes from 6 states. She received a Silver Medal at the competition. Nandi, now age 20, has been involved with Special Olympics Georgia for over 10 years.

Her parents must have given Nandi this determination. They are very active in Special Olympics as well as their community. The Isaac's live two hours away from Atlanta, but travel to Atlanta frequently to attend Council Meetings and bring Nandi to speak. Mrs. Isaac serves on the Governor's Council on Disabilities which meets in Atlanta once a month. This is an important committee which brings people together to discuss policies affecting individuals with disabilities, giving them a voice. Mr. Isaac developed a website for the local Special Olympics program. His website gives important information such as calendars of events, pictures of competitions, referrals for services, and other resources for families.

Nandi is a Global Messenger for Special Olympics Georgia and a trained public speaker. She has spoken to as many as 250 people at the Chief of Police Conventions. Nandi, like her mother, travels frequently to Atlanta for speaking engagements. Recently, she was chosen to participate on the Governor's Partners in Policy Making Committee. Special Olympics Georgia wrote a recommendation for her appointment to this committee. This group meets in Atlanta every other month and trains people with disabilities to be self-advocates. They also teach them how to approach their congressmen to speak on their behalf. During 'Disabilities Awareness Week' in Georgia, Nandi was chosen to serve as a page in the Georgia Senate for a day.

In 2002, the Isaacs were chosen as the Special Olympics Georgia Family of the Year and were honored during the Distinguished Service Awards banquet at the Annual Leadership Conference. During the State Summer Games, the Isaac family was invited to lead the parade of athletes at the Opening Ceremony. This was ideal for a family that brings attention to the needs of people with intellectual disabilities and helps improve their lives—one step at a time.

courage

**Whether it's an art project
or the opportunity to
compete in the Special
Olympics World Games,
Dale will undoubtedly reach
his goal.**

DALE JONES

Dale Jones is an extremely talented artist and dedicated runner from Locust Grove, Georgia. Dale enjoys bowling and basketball. He will readily volunteer to help the First Baptist Church of Locust Grove. Dale also enjoys going into town where he knows many prominent people. Dale not only knows the Mayor and Chief of Police but personally knows the town Fire Chief. The Henry County Board of Commissioners has even recognized Dale.

In 1979, Dale designed the first Special Olympics stamp, which was signed by Eunice Kennedy, founder of Special Olympics Incorporated. Dale continues to enjoy his art. He has sold portraits and seasonal greeting cards through First Baptist Church of Locust Grove. Dale is often asked to design t-shirts for special events for Special Olympics Georgia. For the last three years, he has designed the t-shirts for the annual Sailing Regatta. Dale was asked to design t-shirts for the 2004 Law Enforcement Torch Run.

Dale has been involved with Special Olympics for more than twenty years and attended two Special Olympics World Games competitions. The first was the 1983 Games in Baton Rouge, Louisiana, and then the 1999 Games in Raleigh-Durham, North Carolina. In 1999, he came home with a silver medal in the marathon and a bronze medal in the six mile run. If you ask, he will proudly show off his hard-earned medals. To stay in shape, he runs local 5K and 10K races in Henry County. Dale ran the Peachtree Road Race with a group of athletes and staff from Special Olympics Georgia in 2000.

In May of 2003, Dale was chosen to participate in the Law Enforcement Torch Run at the Special Olympics World Summer Games held in Dublin, Ireland. Those selected, ran all through Europe and Great Britain. Their run began in Greece where the torch was lit from the original eternal flame used in the original Olympic Games. From there, they ran the torch through Turkey, Austria and Central Europe. Next came Belgium where they crossed the Channel to Great Britain. Then onto England, Scotland and the run ended when they reached Ireland. There, they ran the Torch to the Opening Ceremony and lit the cauldron signifying the beginning of the games. There are a limited number of athletes chosen for this run. Each state gets to send only one law enforcement officer as its representative. In addition to the state participants, there are only ten special athletes chosen worldwide to run!

Wow! What a wonderful experience for Dale! He was selected out of all the athletes in the world! Dale was able to experience Europe and became fast friends with the officers. Congratulations to Dale for this great honor! The people and officers Dale met during this exciting experience have brought him wonderful memories for years to come.

Whether it's an art project or the opportunity to compete in the World Games, Dale Jones will undoubtedly reach his goal.

joy

Without Special Olympics, there would be no coaches, no Special Olympics athletes, and just no fun.

44

KELLY KETTLES

Kelly Kettles is a native of Queens, New York. She first participated in Special Olympics in New York at Manhattan College when she was only 11 years old. For the past 18 years, she has traveled across the country meeting people and competing in gymnastics, tennis and basketball. "Special Olympics is a wonderful thing to have in life," Kelly says.

"I participate in Special Olympics for the fun of it! Without it, I might be bored or lonely," says Kelly. "It changed me by helping me to meet new people. I know that Special Olympics is a place where I can just be myself and I can feel comfortable."

It's easy to feel comfortable when you're as good as Kelly. In 1991, she was chosen to go to the Special Olympics World Summer Games in St. Paul, Minnesota. There, she competed in gymnastics, where she did floor exercise, balance beam, the vault and uneven bars. Kelly brought home two gold medals, one bronze medal and a silver medal.

While she no longer competes in gymnastics, Kelly has been playing tennis with Special Olympics for the past nine years. "I love playing tennis because it's fun and it's good exercise – it's a good opportunity to be around people, too" she says.

When she's not at practice, Kelly works as a volunteer for the Cobb County Parks, Recreation and Cultural Affairs Department. She found this position through Special Olympics. There, she files papers, answers phones and makes copies.

When Kelly is not at work or on the basketball or tennis court, she enjoys speaking to large groups about the importance of Special Olympics. As a Global Messenger, Kelly shares stories about her experiences at various competitions and events. She visits schools, civic groups, corporations and other organizations to help educate people on how Special Olympics Georgia has impacted her life. Kelly notes that she enjoys the opportunity to "change people's lives" by telling them about her experiences with Special Olympics Georgia.

Through her travels, Kelly truly has touched many lives. "Sometimes I'll have several people walk up to me, and say that they would like to get involved," Kelly adds. "I tell them we're always looking for more people to join. We need your support because without you – there'd be no coaches, no Special Olympics athletes, and just no fun."

Joey's experiences with Special Olympics Georgia were life changing.

JOEY LANDON

My son, Joey, was first introduced to Special Olympics in the seventh grade. That year he was transferred to Eagle's Landing Middle School. At that time, Joey had been diagnosed with a behavioral disorder called Oppositional Defiant Disorder. I thought Joey's transfer would lead to even more behavioral problems, misunderstandings, and eventually alternative schooling. Before Joey arrived at Eagle's Landing Middle School, he had attended six other schools in other counties and states. At that time, I was not familiar with the Special Olympics program. I speculate that they thought it too risky to consider him for any extracurricular activities because of his unpredictable behavior in public places.

However, this time it was different. His seventh grade teacher happened to be the Henry County Special Olympics coordinator and coach. Even though she quickly learned the magnitude of his sometimes controlling behavior, she would not give up on him, like others had in his past. Joey's behavior would sometimes demand center stage in the classroom. She was determined to help Joey channel that energy toward something positive and rewarding. Joey's experiences with Special Olympics were life-changing.

Joey started out participating in basketball. There were behavioral challenges such as learning and executing good sportsmanship, especially when other teams won. But, there were many valuable lessons that Joey learned while interacting with other athletes. He was continually motivated and soon, Joey was showing major behavioral improvements both inside and outside the classroom. This, from a child who was bounced from psychiatrist to psychologist to a 6-week residential behavior program, all by the tender age of seven.

I know the results achieved through his participation in Special Olympics have had a positive, life-changing effect on Joey. The dedication from caring coaches and loving volunteers has shown remarkable results. Nothing that was tried in the past could do what Special Olympics has done for him. I've often wondered where Joey would be if he hadn't been shown how to positively and constructively channel all of his energy.

Every year through his senior year, Joey participated in sporting events in each of the Fall, Winter, and Summer games. Finally, his behavior was no longer an issue. In fact, he enjoyed helping other athletes. His coordination skills dramatically improved. He matured into a proud Special Olympics athlete. He always looked up to his coach because she courageously saw him through the unique challenges of his disability.

In September 2002, Joey received the Special Olympics Georgia 'Male Athlete of the Year' award. After graduation in June 2003, Joey became an employee at Kroger, and he enjoys it very much. Joey learned team skills in Special Olympics that have carried over into the workplace. When Joey is not working, he continues to participate in sports.

This past year he participated in the Special Olympics equestrian events and alpine skiing in Boone, North Carolina. Joey plays baseball for both the Henry County Recreation, Parks and Services and the Sunshine League baseball team. He also bowls on the Sunshine League bowling team.

Everyone who knows Joey, has been graced at one time or another with his singing. He is a highly motivated choir member at his church. One of Joey's goals is to try to get another gold medal in alpine skiing. He is hopeful that he will get a chance to assist the instructors in teaching the athletes how to tackle those slopes! Joey is loved by everyone he meets; he's a "social butterfly," a definite people person. Who would have ever believed that once his child psychiatrist said Joey was a strong candidate for juvenile delinquency!

There are so many 'Joey's' out there who could benefit from Special Olympics. I just want to thank all the people who dedicate their time and talents to these athletes and the many sponsors who support Special Olympics.

action

The sports that he participates in through Special Olympics Georgia have greatly improved his self-esteem allowing him to grow in his daily life.

STEVE LYONS

Steve Lyons is a true athlete who has enhanced his abilities through his work habits. He is a very fast learner and willing to do whatever it takes to become a better athlete. Steve is full of energy, always has a smile on his face and likes helping others. This past year, Steve participated in powerlifting, softball, basketball, bowling, and volleyball. He has been to every State Games competition since he began Special Olympics at the Kay Center in 1998. Over the years, he has traveled to compete in the Unified Power Partners competition in Maryville, Tennessee, played volleyball in Dallas, Texas, competed in the Georgia Amateur Games, and even entered open weight lifting competitions in Woodstock and Fort Valley, Georgia. In all these competitions, Steve won first place! He continues to lift year-round and assists with powerlifting coaching clinics. Steve has continued to improve in his weight lifting work. He has increased at least one of his lifts in every competition over the last three years. Steve competes in the 170 pound class and deadlifts 380 pounds, bench presses 215 pounds, and squats 225 pounds.

The unified volleyball team that Steve played on won the bronze medal at the 2002 Nationals in Dallas, Texas, and won the gold medal at the State Summer Games at Emory University. Steve played forward on the unified basketball team that participated in a regular season schedule, won gold at Area Winter and Invitational Games. Steve presently bowls every Tuesday and this past year was part of a unified bowling team that won silver at the Unified Masters Tournament.

On the unified softball team, Steve plays second base. He is a key part of the team. Steve and his team played three games this past year against the Fort Valley Utilities Commission, defeating them in all three games. His team won the Invitational in Fort Valley and received a bronze at the State Fall Games.

Steve's past accomplishments also include: competing and winning in open powerlifting competitions, two time winner at the Georgia Amateur Games, winner in the Savannah weight lifting competition, three time Power Partners winner in Tennessee, member of 1998 Arizona and 2002 Dallas, Texas, Volleyball team, participated in the Atlanta Braves and Hawks Clinics, and NesSmith Special Olympics Male Basketball Player of the Year.

Presently, Steve is working at Kay Center with the landscaping crew. He works Monday through Friday and is always willing to assist around the center after working hours. Steve completes his daily powerlifting each morning, and he is a great help with the elderly that live around him assisting with raking yards and mowing grass. Steve is now living on his own and likes to assist with basketball and powerlifting clinics. The Special Olympics sports that he has participated in have greatly improved his self-esteem allowing him to grow in his daily life.

courage

These Special Olympics games and the daily practices are preparing him for regular competitions.

Louis Maxwell

Louis Maxwell is a 22 year old from Fort Valley, Georgia. Louis has only been lifting weights for a couple of years but he has accomplished a great deal.

He has lifted over 580 pounds and placed first just about every time he has competed. His personal best is 585 in the dead lift, 275 in the bench press and 341 in the squat. At the Southeast Regional Powerlifting Competition, Louis was the overall champion lifting a total of 1072 pounds, beating out 79 other competitors.

Kay Center has a weight room where 25 of the clients work out. Louis says, "The weight room is the place I go when I get depressed. It's cool to be able to work out in there." He loves to compete and he takes his Special Olympics competitions very seriously.

His powerlifting coach said, "The ultimate goal is to get him into an open, or regular, weightlifting competition." These Special Olympics Georgia games and training are preparing him for regular competitions. He also said this program helps integrate special athletes into their communities. People from the community come in and work out and offer advice to Louis and others who lift in the weight room.

joy

Now, it is my turn!

MEGAN BENSMAN

Megan Bensman is an 18-year-old Special Olympics Georgia athlete that is truly an inspiration. I have watched her grow over the past six years into a fantastic young lady. Megan entered my classroom in her 6th grade year. This was her first year in middle school and she was absolutely fearful of what would come over the next three years. She was a shy, quiet, young lady that had just been placed into a self-contained special education setting.

Megan struggled for several years in a regular classroom environment with some resource class assistance for learning disabilities. She was re-tested and found to be intellectually disabled which required more assistance. Megan's parents were told that "a self-contained setting would be more beneficial." They were told Megan would not be able to learn very much and classes would become harder as she progressed.

I am a believer in "I can." I teach individuals they have to prove to me that they "can't." Thank goodness, it did not take me long to convince Megan of that theory. If you ask her she will tell you, "I can do anything I want to do." She believes it and she achieves it.

Megan does have difficulty reading. As a matter of fact, it is by far her greatest disability, but we did not focus on that. We focused on what Megan's strengths were and intertwined reading with these strengths. You see, if you focus on strengths, you build the weaknesses.

Megan has three older sisters who have always been involved with band and other activities throughout their school careers. Megan had been in my class for about five months when I asked her if she would like to attend the Special Olympics Georgia State Indoor Winter Games as a bowler. Her answer was immediately, "Yes! Finally, a chance for me to do something that my sisters cannot do." She then asked me if it would be all right if her family came to watch her. When I told her yes, she immediately came out of her shyness and quietness. She said, "I have always had to go to everything my sisters have done and now it is my turn!"

The whole family has been there every time Megan has competed in an event. Whether it was local, area, state, or even world games, some, if not all of Megan's family have been there to support her. Megan was even selected to attend the 2003 Special Olympics World Summer Games in Dublin, Ireland, as part of the Special Olympics Georgia Women's Volleyball Team. And yes, her entire family, including her grandmother went to Ireland to support Megan.

Megan has been a very loyal employee at Kroger for the past two years and is very faithful to her job. When I asked her to go with me to the lake to ride the Sea-Doo she stated, "You just have to let me know two weeks ahead of time so I can ask off work."

Megan continues to attend local, area, and state games in a variety of sports. She works on the weekends when she is not competing. She hangs out with her friends and participates in most normal 18-year-old activities. I am glad Megan believes in herself. If you ask her about having a disability she will tell you, "I can do whatever I want to do. So what, I can't do some things. I can do some things that other people cannot even do." What an inspiration!

inspire

Matt is a good man, with a huge heart, and a love for everything and everyone around him.

MATT MCWHORTER

I first met Matt in 1998 when I starting working for Resources and Residential Alternatives. He was doing his usual rounds asking people what music they wanted on their mix tapes. Matt has a love for music that extends across genre. Country, rap, pop, classical, you name it, and he'll find something he likes. He rounded the corner and there he was in my doorway. "Well, I'm not much for country, but surprise me!" I say.

"Sure thing, I'll let you know when it's ready."

"Thanks!" I say, we both smile and he continues rolling from door to door. A few days later, Matt's back in my doorway, tape in hand smiling. "Here it is. I hope you like it!" I took the tape and thanked him. Not having a cassette player in my car, it was a few days before I had a chance to listen to it. I put it in one night while making dinner at home. The first song on the tape was Shania Twain, one of his favorites. Despite my hint that I wasn't into country, he put it on that tape because he knew what most people tend to forget, trying something once can open up a world of opportunity. I surprised myself by liking that song. I liked the whole tape. It hasn't turned me into a country fan, but I now find myself stopping to listen to a good country song from time to time, something I never would have done before. More importantly, that tape made me stop and really look at Matt. What I saw is a good man, with a huge heart, and a love for everything and everyone around him.

Matt came to Resources and Residential Alternatives in 1992. He lived in the East Hembree Group Home for many years, but has since moved to another group Home where he lives with 3 other men. He worked at Herman Miller manufacturing high-end office furniture. Once the factory closed, Matt landed his dream job, working part-time during the holidays as a greeter for Media Play. He loves the opportunity to spend all day immersed in music. During the rest of the year, Matt works for the organization and will soon be working in their liquidation store.

Being involved with Special Olympics Georgia has offered Matt yet another set of opportunities. As an athlete, he medaled in wheelchair racing and discovered his new favorite sport, bowling. Matt uses the off season to strengthen his game. He spread the mission of Special Olympics Georgia as a Global Messenger and found that public speaking was a venue where he could truly inspire others.

Matt enjoys public speaking. You may meet him one day at a fundraiser, a public school, or a professional conference, sharing his life experiences as a person with a disability. Matt assists the RRA staff by training them about self-determination, as well as other topics.

Matt stays close to his family, visiting as often as his busy schedule allows. One of his favorite subjects to talk about is his brother, Chris. Matt and I have talked many times about Chris' trials and tribulations on the way to becoming a doctor. On the day Chris wed, Matt was pleased to be one of his groomsman and is now a proud uncle. He hopes that one day Chris will stand with him when he marries Lisa, the love of his life.

I have moved on from Resources and Residential Alternatives, and my life doesn't allow me to talk to Matt as much as I used to. But, I doubt that he will ever stop setting and achieving his goals. By giving himself to the world, he is assured of never ending success and by opening himself to me, he gave me the gift of opportunity.

action

She faces any new
challenge with
confidence now.

CASEY BRENNAN

Casey is a very pleasant, petite young lady with a great attitude. She is always quick with her smile, and has never met a stranger. She has been employed at Publix since 1996.

Since 1989, she has participated in swimming, diving, tennis, equestrian, bowling, volleyball, softball and ice skating. Casey has always been very small. Consequently, people have a tendency to treat her as a younger child and not expect much from her.

Before Special Olympics, she was content to lay back and get by with as little as possible. Special Olympics has brought her out of her shell and has been instrumental in developing her into a proud young adult.

Casey is not pushed to participate in sports. Her parents support her, but her drive comes completely from within. Casey does well in all her sports; it's amazing to watch her pitch on her softball team. But, ice-skating is *her* sport. In addition to her practice sessions, you will find her practicing her routines quietly in her room when she is alone. She chooses her own music, costumes, and has very definite opinions on what and how to do her skating programs.

On average, she works about six months on the two-minute program. Watch closely during the two minutes she is on ice, and you will see a person demonstrating that she has accomplished everything she set out to do. During these two minutes, Casey has enough adrenaline to make her raise the bar for her next ice-skating event. Thus, she will immediately start over for the next six months. She does this twelve months a year, all the while participating in her other sports and activities.

Through Special Olympics, she has learned how to set goals and to accomplish them through hard work. Her activities have developed her physically, mentally and emotionally. She understands the value and the need for "practice, practice, practice" and applies this to every facet of her life. She faces any new challenge with confidence now. Casey is a very capable young lady, but before Special Olympics this was anything but the case. Casey is now taking on the responsibility to give back to the program that has helped her so much by speaking in public on behalf of the organization as a Global Messenger.

Casey speaks of her accomplishments to companies and at various events. Most of the time the audience is surprised with her level of success. No one can build this awareness better than the athletes of Special Olympics. Casey has accepted this leadership role to inspire and educate the public as a way to show her appreciation for this great organization.

courage

My life is richer because of Special Olympics Georgia and my friendship with Lee.

LEE PALMER

The definition of "athlete" is a person possessing the natural or acquired traits, such as strength, agility, and endurance that are necessary for physical exercise or sports, especially those performed in competitive contexts. Lee Palmer weighs 380 pounds and appears to be the farthest away from anyone's idea of an athlete. Yet, that's exactly what he is—an athlete.

Lee has been involved in Special Olympics Georgia for eight years. He is all that the Special Olympics ideal embodies. He is courageous in his attempts at softball, volleyball, bowling and floor hockey and is the team leader. He doesn't look like someone who could even run around the bases but he manages very well. He likes to win but also accepts loss as part of the whole picture.

Nothing says more about him than this incident that happened at the Special Olympics Georgia State Winter Games Floor Hockey Competition. During one of the games, we played a team whose players were tiny compared to our much larger guys. However, this team was not intimidated and gave everything they had. In the excitement of playing, Lee turned around and bumped into one of the other team's players, knocking him to the floor. The referee immediately blew his whistle and indicated that Lee would be going to the penalty box. The first thing Lee did was to turn to the other player, who was lying on the floor, and extend his hand to him. He picked him up off the floor and the auditorium burst out cheering! I have the benefit of knowing that Lee would not have done that on purpose, but the referee called it as he saw it. Lee took his penalty minutes without complaining and got right back in the game.

If Lee is aware of a need for the team, he manages to do everything within his power to meet that need. He has helped raise money for equipment and is an excellent spokesperson for the team and Special Olympics Georgia. He has many friends and makes friends with everyone he meets. I am proud to call him my friend.

Special Olympics Georgia has given Lee, and other athletes like him, opportunities to excel in ways that they never had before. Instead of coming up short, they are the stars. They have also learned about pride in doing something well - acceptance and recognition for a job well done. Many skills have been learned as well. Lee has carried the team flag in the opening ceremony and has led the masses in the Athlete's Oath. He has never had a chance to stand before a group that large and lead anything before. Can those of us who have never been afforded these opportunities truly understand what that meant to him?

I am so thankful for having Lee as a friend and being able to participate with him and others in Special Olympics Georgia. My life is richer because of Special Olympics Georgia and my friendship with Lee.

joy

...she is the epitome of
what Special Olympics
stands for: Sharing,
Joy and Courage.

RUDOLPHA RICHARDS

Special Olympics welcomed a truly inspiring person into the world on September 29, 1978, in St. Thomas, Virgin Islands. Her name is Rudolpha Richards, and she is the epitome of what Special Olympics stands for: Sharing, Joy, and Courage. Twenty-five years later, she has taken her life to levels she never knew possible, all with the help of Special Olympics.

Rudolpha has been participating in Special Olympics for well over ten years. Beginning in the Virgin Islands, her first love was tennis. Her coach, who wanted to get tennis started in their area, asked Rudolpha to try this challenging racquet sport. Although she was hesitant because she didn't know the rules and had never played, she quickly grew to love the sport. In fact, she loved it so much that when she attended her first competition, Rudolpha took home the gold for the Virgin Islands. From there, her passion for Special Olympics really took off. She became more involved with the program. Rudolpha became a spokesperson for the Board of Directors in the Virgin Islands. As a spokesperson, she sat with the Board to give her input on the decisions that were being made for the organization from an athlete's perspective.

Throughout St. Thomas, Rudolpha was quickly becoming a celebrity as she traveled around helping with fundraisers. In her travels, Rudolpha worked to spread the word of Special Olympics. Her continued involvement in the program led her to the 1999 Special Olympics World Summer Games in Raleigh, North Carolina. She competed in tennis once again. There, she was the recipient of a silver medal for Women's Doubles and a bronze medal for Mixed Doubles. While playing tennis, she always aspired to be like her favorite sports celebrities: Venus and Serena Williams.

After living in St. Thomas all of her life, she and her mother moved to Atlanta, Georgia, in 2000. Immediately, Rudolpha became involved in the DeKalb and Gwinnett County Special Olympics Georgia programs. Over the years, she has competed in many sports: basketball, volleyball, bowling, softball, and most recently, Alpine skiing. In fact, in June of 2003, she went to her THIRD World Games in Dublin, Ireland, with her volleyball team. All of her coaches speak very highly of her, saying that Rudolpha is a born leader. In fact, when she was in Ireland, some mornings she would be up before her coaches to help her teammates get ready for the long day ahead.

Rudolpha is incredibly well-rounded and participates in many activities outside of competing with Special Olympics. She has had a job for the last four years at Hands for Hire, where she is an administrative assistant. Her main duties are filing, giving out paperwork, and (her favorite part) socializing with her two managers. Rudolpha enjoys this job very much because she loves to meet new people and even spreads the word to her co-workers about what Special Olympics is all about.

Becoming a Global Messenger for Special Olympics Georgia, according to Rudolpha, was definitely an exciting and inspirational time for her. In 2003, she took a class that gave her tips on how to speak in front of large groups while sharing her joy for Special Olympics Georgia. This gave her the confidence to speak to large groups, such as Georgia State University. She often talks about her experiences growing up in the Virgin Islands. She compares the program from home and to the program here in Georgia, saying that the focus in Georgia is very community oriented. This is unlike St. Thomas, where the government wasn't very supportive of Special Olympics, therefore stalling the program from growth.

Rudolpha is just like any typical 25-year-old woman. Her favorite things to do are have fun, meet new people, and spread her enthusiasm of Special Olympics. She loves to cook, and her specialties are fried plantains, cakes, and macaroni and cheese. Rudolpha especially likes to spend time with her fiancé, whom she met while playing softball with the DeKalb County Angels. She insists that it was love at first sight and the wedding is set for June 16, 2007. Rudolpha's truest hero in life is her 'Mommy.' "She is a very strong woman and always supports what I want to do," says Rudolpha.

Rudolpha is the strongest person she can be because of support from family and friends while she pursues her dreams through Special Olympics. The Special Olympics Georgia program is lucky to have such a giving, genuinely caring person to spread its word.

inspire

Katie believes in herself the way we all should – with a quiet air of confidence that she is doing her personal best.

KATIE ROUILLE

Katie is 22 years old and has lived in Tucker, Georgia, her whole life. She has the wisdom and life perspective of someone twice her age. Katie has two brothers and unbelievable parents. They support her in every way. Her mom is always helping at the Special Olympics office. She helps plan family activities and assists with Global Messenger activities and training. It's no wonder Katie is as optimistic and genuinely happy as she is. Her family is the same way. The first thing you will notice about Katie is not her disability; it's her huge smile! Katie has never greeted me without that smile.

At first glance, Katie is like many other young women – she likes to watch television, listen to country music and talk on the phone. She works at a local Publix Supermarket, gathering carts and doing other jobs. She works long hours, but doesn't complain. In fact, she said her co-workers complain about their long hours to her, but she just says, "Relax, it's just work." That attitude is ever present in Katie. It's one of the many things about her that makes her an inspiration. Some of Katie's other achievements include: being a current member of the Special Olympics Georgia Board of Directors, a former Special Olympics Georgia intern, a graduate of Tucker High School, and an actress with the Habima Community Theatre.

She's a gold medal winner in both aquatics and volleyball. In fact, she's been to the World Games twice! First, in 1999 for aquatics in North Carolina, where she won two gold medals and one silver. Then in 2003 for volleyball in Ireland. In Ireland, Katie's team competed against teams from India, Mexico, Japan and Tennessee.

When I asked Katie about her favorite part of her trip to Ireland she said, "Pulling pranks on my coaches with my teammates." Not, the sight-seeing or the fact that now she's been to Europe – the things many people might value most. Instead, Katie remembers and appreciates the experiences and laughter she shared with her close friends and leaders.

Katie is a hero and she knows it. She's not a bragger or a boaster, just self-assured. Katie believes in herself the way we all should – with a quiet air of confidence that she is doing her personal best. As she put it, "I'm a great hero. I do sports so that someday someone will look up to me like I do to my coaches. It's all about how you live life. Just live life to the fullest."

action

**The unifying power of love
and support is paramount to
our well being and Special
Olympics athletes seem to
understand the dynamics of it
better than most.**

BRYAN RUFF

Bryan Ruff is 21 years old and brings a smile to everyone's face wherever he goes. Bryan is a terrific athlete who attended the 2003 Special Olympics World Summer Games in Dublin, Ireland, as part of Team USA/Georgia. Even though Bryan was ecstatic about the World Games, I knew something had to be done when he asked if his face would look like "this" (pulling his skin back tight to his face) when the airplane took off. This 20-year-old had cartoon images of airplane travel. That's when I made reservations for the two of us to fly a turn around flight from Atlanta to Orlando.

On the way to the airport, Bryan's questions were many but mostly he was excited. I asked several times, "Bryan, are you nervous?" He responded each time with, "No, I'm not nervous, but my legs are anxious." He was somewhat surprised that everything seemed normal, just like it would if you were sitting in school or driving in a car. Once at cruising altitude, the flight attendant came by to ask if we would like a drink and some pretzels. Bryan politely told her he didn't like pretzels and then asked, "Do you have any fudge rounds?" Letting Bryan know that she did not have fudge rounds, she did offer some cookies, which he accepted along with a can of Coke. Finding out this was Bryan's first plane trip, the crew gave him his "wings" which he wore proudly.

On the return flight, Bryan was confident and proud. Without any hesitation he made sure he was provided the cookies and the entire can of Coke. Recognizing the "wings" he was wearing, the new flight attendant inquired about the reasons for his flight. "I'm Bryan Ruff and I'm going to the Special Olympics World Summer Games in Dublin, Ireland, to run the 1/2 marathon this summer and this is my practice flight." Intrigued, she left and returned with pen and paper to get the "rest of the story" of this famous Special Olympics athlete. Certainly not the shy one, Bryan offered her many details of his impending trip to Ireland. Bursting with pride, he became an ambassador for Special Olympics in this spontaneous interview.

Later, as our airplane taxied toward our gate in Atlanta, the flight attendant's voice could be heard giving connecting flight information, etc. Then, we heard her say, "I'd like to have everyone's attention for an announcement. We have a special guest traveling with us today. His name is Bryan Ruff from Athens, Georgia, and he will be representing Team USA at the Special Olympics World Summer Games in Dublin, Ireland, this summer. He will be competing in the 1/2 marathon with a preliminary time of 1 hour and 47 minutes. This is his maiden flight in preparation for the travel he will be doing this summer to attend those games. We are extremely proud to have him on board with us today and we all wish him lots of success as he represents Team USA." As she finished, cheers and applause erupted from the passengers. At 6 foot 4 inches, Bryan is easy to recognize and he acknowledged their response with a 'parade' wave and a smile as big as the entire outdoors.

A plane full of strangers, just wanting to get on with their lives with as little interruption, interaction and delay as possible, suddenly came alive with smiles, handshakes and congratulations. Almost everyone lingered a few extra moments to wish him the best. The unifying power of love and support is paramount to our well being and Special Olympics athletes seem to understand the dynamics of it better than most. Giving of themselves so naturally makes the world a better work place. The smile, the acknowledgement and the wave is just one example of Special Olympics athletes putting their love out there and having others respond in kind.

At the World Games, Bryan received a silver medal in the 3,000 meter race with a time of 12:00 minutes and fifth place in the half marathon with a time of 1 hour 44 minutes 46 seconds. His positive attitude and happy demeanor only surpass Bryan's dedication to his training. Bryan's success is even more inspirational when you look into his past and understand that he comes from a foster home with five other children. Bryan has had to depend on himself and motivate himself to succeed as his foster parents had little time to cheer for Bryan. Bryan participates in Special Olympics with Athens/Clarke County and has some great support from his coaches.

She relates all her success as a person to the many benefits that Special Olympics Georgia has bestowed upon her.

Lori Santos

Lori Santos, an athlete from Valdosta, Georgia, has competed in Special Olympics for the last 12 years. She participates in bowling, equestrian, athletics, volleyball, and bocce. There have been many exciting moments for her over the past few years. If you were to ask Lori, about her greatest and fondest moment in Special Olympics, she would say, without a doubt, it was when she was chosen to attend World Games in 1999. She competed in bocce. Lori knew that it would be hard work and with a "good coach" as she states, she couldn't help but do her best and achieve at the highest level. Lori knew it wasn't all about winning but about doing the very best she could do.

She stated that her coach would always tell her to relax and enjoy the game. Encouragement from her coach helped her to become less tense. She knew that all the hard work and practice would soon pay off. After several months of practicing, Lori and all of Team USA boarded a plane to Raleigh, North Carolina. The ride in the jet was exciting. Lori was able to overcome her fears and enjoy conversations with the pilot and flight attendants on board.

She's a very confident athlete, ready to take on the world. Lori has met so many athletes from other countries and traded pins with them. Her coach was so proud of the athlete she had become even before the competition. Lori won the gold medal in the Singles competition and teaming up with a partner from North Georgia they won the silver in the Doubles competition.

After returning from the Special Olympics World Summer Games in 1999, she received the Proclamation to the City of Valdosta from the Mayor for all of her hard work and dedication to the competition. She will never forget the moment she was handed the Proclamation and that day will always be remembered as 'Lori Santos Day.'

Lori works part-time at Applebee's Restaurant in her hometown. She loves her job and likes working with everyone. She enjoys cleaning and taking care of the restaurant. She has been employed with the company for over 8 years. She spends any free time with friends and taking walks in her neighborhood. Lori also participates with the Recreation Department in leisure activities, and attends Morningside Baptist Church.

She owns her home and also enjoys working in her yard on pretty days. She says Special Olympics is fun, and it's all right if you do not win medals, it gives you a chance to meet and socialize with friends. One of her favorite sports, besides bocce of course, is equestrian. She has had the opportunity to travel and compete at the state level. She enjoys all the work it takes to get the horse ready to compete.

Lori is always excited about getting out her cleaning box and brushing the horses. Some of the events she enjoys at the Recreation Department are social dances, swimming, volleyball, crafts, musicals, movies, game night, and so much more. She relates all her success as a person to the many benefits that Special Olympics Georgia has bestowed upon her. She has gained self-confidence, and self worth – and those qualities help her get through all of life's challenges.

joy

Loren is a loyal friend, and someone who can teach us about the positive side of life.

LOREN SMITH

Loren Smith is a 29-year-old adult Special Olympics Georgia athlete. He participates at the Henry County Parks & Recreation Department in McDonough, Georgia. According to his mother, he has been active in Special Olympics for 14 years. Loren first started through the Henry County School System. He has participated in several sports, but unified softball is his favorite. One of his mom's proudest moments occurred last year when Loren made two runs during the Henry County Special Olympics Georgia Softball Invitational. He had never made two runs in one game before. The moment was a very emotional one, for both of Loren's parents. His father was led to tears.

Loren's coach shared that Loren knows how to win a crowd and "is always smiling and portraying a positive attitude." All agree that he is a very caring and kind person, "His personality shines and makes others feel good when they're around him." Loren's parents shared the importance of exposing Loren to his community and social activities. They wanted him to be comfortable with himself and with others. This goal has been obtained in part, because of his participation in Special Olympics. Loren's strong social skills were also partly gained from his full time job at the Henry County Medical Center. He had worked in the Environmental Services Department for seven years, but he unfortunately had to quit last year due to medical problems.

Loren is better now, and working part time at a local Papa John's Restaurant. When Loren's coach was asked about his past medical problems, she shared that Loren was "very strong and determined to fight through his health problems so he would not miss a beat with the Henry County Parks and Recreation programs." He was a "trooper and never once complained about his illness." As soon as Loren was back on his feet, he made sure that he came to the Special Olympics events to support his friends.

To all that know him, Loren is a loyal friend and someone who can teach us all about the positive side of life.

Elena has never really known "can't."

ELENA WEAVER

Elena Weaver is 23 years old. She is very happy and healthy. Elena is also an active participant in Special Olympics Georgia. Her chosen sport for the last 6 years is artistic gymnastics; and she has excelled both mentally and physically in her sport! Every year, at the state games, she brings home the gold!

Elena's life had a very difficult beginning. She spent many years in and out of hospitals and doctor's offices. She endured multiple surgeries, tests and therapies that would eventually provide her with the opportunity to be an active participant in society. Her doctors have deemed her a "medical miracle" with a will to survive and a desire to accomplish high goals.

Every time Elena encounters a new skill in her training, she will spend time thinking, planning, working and believing that she can do the skill. Many times, her friends, family and teachers have told her, "It's okay, look at all you have accomplished. It's okay if you can't do the skill." She just smiles and then becomes the best she can be at what others say "she can't do."

Elena has never really known "can't." When we think she has hit her "maximum" in life— she just keeps on climbing that mountain! At this point, those of us who know her best are learning to let Elena lead us onto the next adventure.

Speaking of adventures, in 2003 Elena joined a group of Cobb County Special Olympics gymnasts to perform at the 12th World Gymnaestrada in Portugal, Spain. They performed before 24,000 athletes from 52 countries. The family shed many tears that night. Elena's goal has always been to become a "world-class gymnast!" We patted her shoulder and said, "that's a nice goal" — we just knew it was impossible. Elena believed - worked hard - prayed hard - and we followed her to Europe as she accomplished this dream. On the trip home, she quietly whispered to us, "Well, now I'm a world-class gymnast." She's also a world-class person!

Elena has been encouraged to do more for Special Olympics. She is an active Global Messenger, having written and delivered many speeches to civic and law enforcement groups. This year will be her fourth year to "run the torch" for Georgia Law Enforcement as they raise money for the State Games. When the Georgia cops spend a weekend on top of donut shops as a fundraiser — she is there to perform her gymnastics and help raise money. However, the activity she enjoyed most was her volunteer position in the Special Olympics.

She is very outgoing and has never met a stranger.

SUSAN WILDER

Susan has been competing in Special Olympics Georgia since 1984. She is currently an active participant at age 28. As an athlete she participates in aquatics, equestrian, bowling, bocce, ice skating, golf skills, artistic roller skating, table tennis, and athletics. She has participated in local, area, state, regional and world games. Since being involved with Special Olympics she has won several bronze, silver and gold medals. She also has been named the Area 6 Athlete of the Year.

In 1995, she was chosen to go to the Special Olympics World Summer Games in New Haven, Connecticut, as an artistic roller skater. At the world games, she won two gold medals and one bronze medal. Mr. Ted Kennedy, Jr. presented one of the gold medals to her. Upon arriving home from the World Games, she was welcomed with a surprise party by friends, relatives and neighbors. Also at her party were local television, newspaper and radio stations ready to interview her. Susan is well liked in her hometown of Griffin, Georgia. She is very outgoing and has never met a stranger. In 1996, she was chosen to carry the Olympic Torch in Griffin before the 1996 Special Olympics Summer Games in Atlanta.

Susan is a big help at home with many different chores. She especially likes to help take care of her six-month-old nephew, Jacob, who loves her dearly. Susan always tries to do her best and is quick to learn.

As her mother and coach in some of her sports, I am so very proud of all her accomplishments. As parents of children with intellectual disabilities, we sometimes get frustrated or impatient. I just try to remember that God gave us these precious ones to care for because He knew we could. He gives us the strength and understanding.

courage

It was a shaky start to what would become an unforgettable journey.

ROBERT WILLIAMSON

Robert is a 57-year-old Special Olympics athlete from Savannah, Georgia. When he walked into the Anderson-Cohen Weightlifting Center a few years ago, his coach wasn't sure if he'd ever be able to lift weights, much less compete. Severe osteoporosis prevented Robert from lifting much of anything. His coach said, "I was wondering if he'd ever really be able to be part of a power lifting team and compete."

Even the smallest dumbbell was too much for Robert to lift. In fact, the most he could handle was a small, two-and-a-half pound weight. It was a shaky start to what would become an unforgettable journey. "It wasn't long before he surprised every one of us," said his coach. "He never ceases to amaze me."

Robert trains at the Anderson-Cohen Center twice a week to lift weights alongside United States Olympic weightlifting hopefuls. He now bypasses the smaller weights. After years of hard work and perseverance, he can dead lift 200 pounds and bench-press 70 pounds. "It's just incredible," said Langford. "He has come such a long way."

Robert has the hardware to prove it. "I've got a whole room full of medals," said Robert. The weightlifting program has not only helped Robert increase his strength and coordination, but it also gives him a real purpose. "It has helped him a lot," said Robert's legal guardian. "It's something he looks forward to, and it's a great program and outlet for the athletes."

His guardian said she can see the difference the weightlifting program has made in Robert. "Sometimes, improvement isn't just lifting more weights. "Sometimes, improvement is your attitude and being happy when you finish what you're doing." But Robert isn't the only one benefiting. Those who watch and work with Robert say that it is his *inner* strength that consistently shines through and inspires those around him. "He is just a joy for all of us to be around. There's not a soul that's ever met him who's going to forget him."

joy

My dream came true when I gave the athletes their medals at the awards ceremony. It made me so happy!

KATY WILSON

Katy Wilson has been involved in Special Olympics Georgia for over 18 years. She started participating in Special Olympics when she was only six years old. Even though she was too young to compete, she carried the banner into the stadium at the State Summer Games at Emory University. Katy was so small that she could barely see over the top of the banner. Luckily, her cowboy hat was very big so everyone could see her!

Later she competed in athletics, and won her first gold medal! Now, she has won over 100 medals and ribbons, and they are all hanging in her bedroom!

When Katy was born, she was very tiny and weak. She suffered with heart problems and had very weak muscles. Katy could not hold her head up or even move around on the floor. Her family and coaches worked hard with her. They did NOT GIVE UP! They said, "We can do this together." Now, she is strong and healthy, and Special Olympics gives her the confidence to reach her goals. Special Olympics is an important part of Katy's life!

In 1999, she went to the Special Olympics World Summer Games in Raleigh, North Carolina. There, she competed in all the gymnastics events—bars, balance beam, vault, and floor exercise. She won two gold medals! Olympic champions, Nadia Comaneci and Bart Conner, were there and Katy was able to meet them. They said she did the most beautiful cartwheels they had ever seen! The next year she was invited to perform with the T.J. Maxx Tour of Gymnastics Champions in Reno, Nevada and Atlanta, Georgia. She performed a beam routine with Shannon Miller in Philips Arena. Katy said, "when I did my handstand and dismount off the beam, everyone stood up and cheered for me! I was so happy—and people asked ME for my autograph! It was really fun!"

Katy is also a Global Messenger for Special Olympics Georgia. She travels and makes speeches so that people can learn more about Special Olympics. Some of the trips Katy has taken are to Alaska, California, New York, Chicago, Canada, and the Netherlands. She has also been invited to the White House twice! At the White House, Katy met President and Mrs. Bush and President and Mrs. Clinton. "When I held out my hand to President Bush, he said, "Katy, I don't want a handshake—I need a hug!" "He told me he was very proud of me!", Katy said.

In 2003, she went to the Special Olympics World Summer Games in Ireland as a special guest of Mrs. Eunice Kennedy Shriver. Katy said, "My dream was to give out medals and ribbons to the other athletes. Bart Conner was the Master of Ceremonies at the gymnastics venue, and he invited me to help him." As special guest, Katy welcomed everyone, and spoke to the athletes and their families. She wished everyone, Good Luck! Katy admits, "My dream came true when I gave the athletes their medals at the awards ceremony. It made me so happy!"

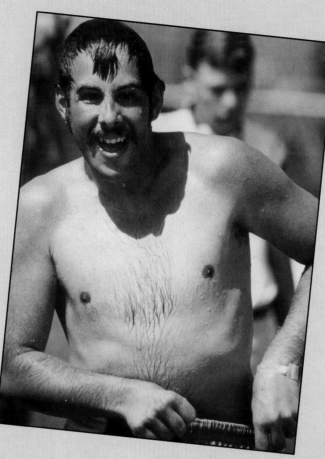